Mommy
Drinks

Because You Cry

You Probably Need This One, Too

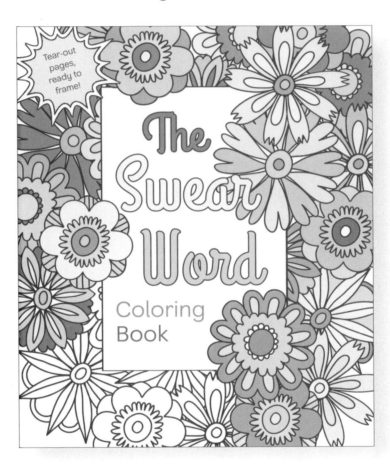

Tear-out pages, ready to frame!

The Swear Word Coloring Book

Mommy Drinks
Because You Cry

A Sarcastic
Coloring Book

ST. MARTIN'S GRIFFIN
NEW YORK

ZENDOODLE COLORING PRESENTS MOMMY DRINKS BECAUSE YOU CRY

Copyright © 2016 by St. Martin's Press. All rights reserved.

Printed in the United States of America. For information, address
St. Martin's Press, 175 Fifth Avenue, New York, N.Y. 10010.

www.stmartins.com

ISBN 978-1-250-11991-9 (trade paperback)

Our books may be purchased in bulk for promotional, educational,
or business use. Please contact your local bookseller or the
Macmillan Corporate and Premium Sales Department at
1-800-221-7945, extension 5442, or by e-mail
at MacmillanSpecialMarkets@macmillan.com.

First Edition: April 2016

10 9 8 7 6

"Trust me, you can dance."

—Vodka

How about never?
Is never good for you?

BE NICE TO YOUR CHILDREN,
FOR THEY WILL CHOOSE
YOUR RETIREMENT HOME.

Remember when I asked
for your opinion?
Yeah, me neither.

I'm eating
my feelings
and they're
absolutely
delicious.

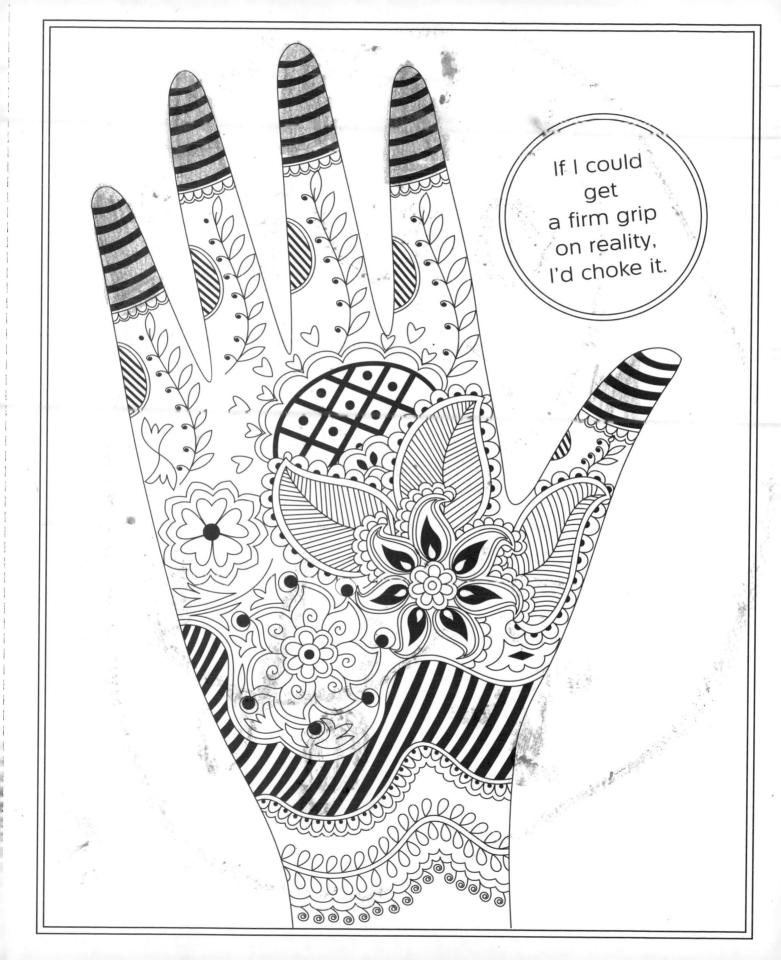

If I could
get
a firm grip
on reality,
I'd choke it.

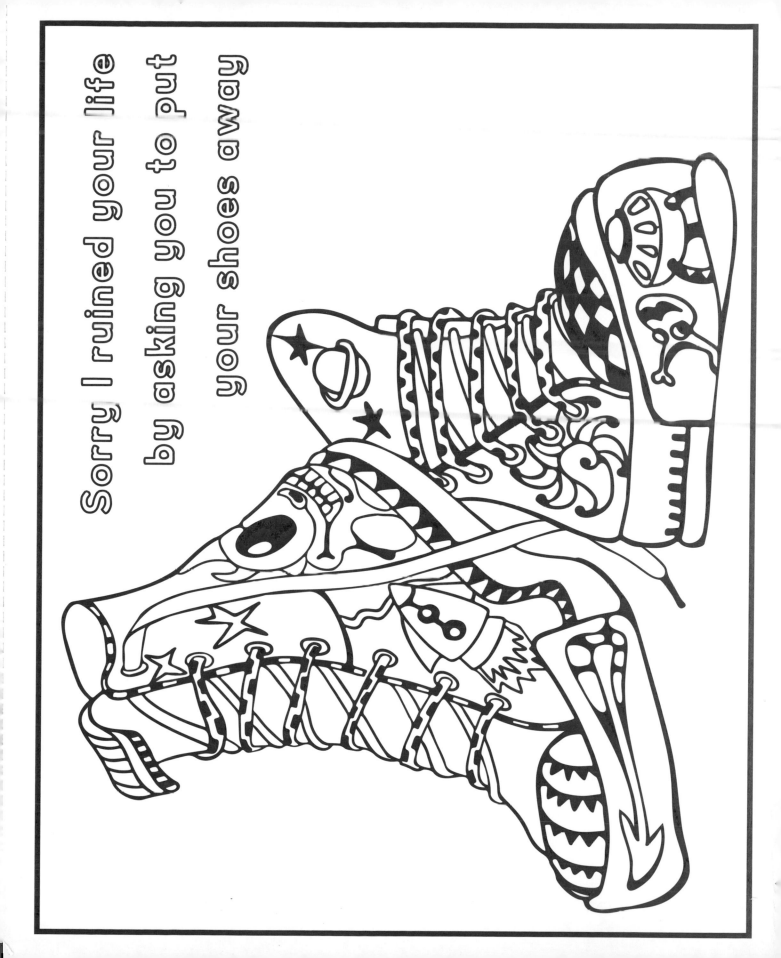

Today's Mood: Bitch with a chance of sarcasm

I plan to love you, nurture you, and give you enough dysfunction to make you funny.

8 hours of labor means I'm always right.

I love cleaning up messes I didn't make,
so I became a mom.

Your
wedding plans
sound really
interesting
to you.

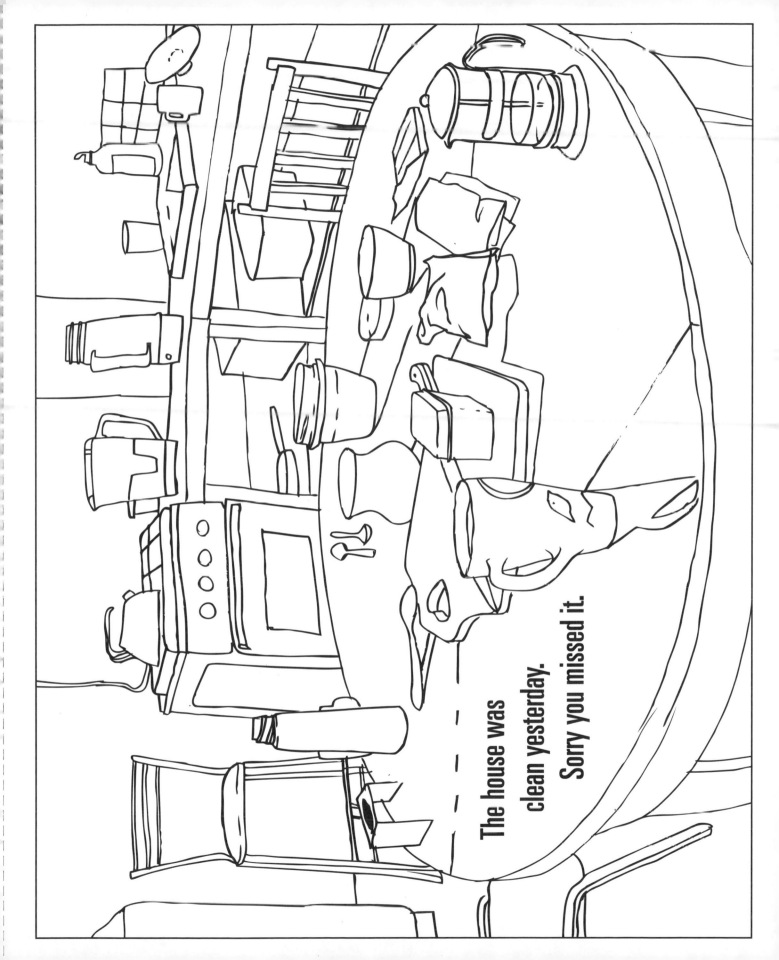

The house was
clean yesterday.
Sorry you missed it.

I child-proofed the house, but they still get in.

You
deplete
me

MY IDEA OF A HAPPY MEAL IS A BOTTLE OF VODKA, 2 XANAX AND A COOKIE

Another fine day
ruined by responsibility.

DON'T MAKE ME ROLL MY EYES!

I hear you. I'm just not listening.

I have mixed drinks about feelings

YOU ARE ABOUT TO EXCEED
THE LIMITS OF MY MEDICATION

Let's pretend I give a shit and leave it at that.

I'm feeling a bit overworked and under-intoxicated.

Home is where the vodka is